GARY JONES

Santorini Travel Guide

First edition

This book was professionally typeset on Reedsy.
Find out more at reedsy.com

Contents

Introduction

Santorini is a favorite destination – not just for people in Greece but also for people all over the world. Unfortunately, there are so many places and things to do in Santorini that even planning a vacation to the island can be a lot of work.

Where do you go first?

What food should you taste?

What should you do?

By the end of this book, you should have fairly good idea of what to do and the places to visit in Santorini for a truly satisfying vacation.

1

Brief History and Background

Santorini is rumored to be the location of the famous City of Atlantis – and it's not surprising why. The island is actually a remnant of a volcanic caldera – which makes it amazing in itself. A volcanic caldera is essentially a volcanic crater that was formed after an eruption, causing the mouth of the volcano to collapse.

Found in the Southern Portion of the Aegean Sea, Santorini forms part of the Cyclades group of islands. What's interesting here is that while the island is globally known as "Santorini", its official name is actually Thera or Thira – hence the Airport in the island is called the Thira International Airport.

The municipality of Santorini is comprised of 6 islands. There's Santorini and Therasia – both of which are inhabited. Three of the islands are uninhabited which include Nea Kameni, Palaia Kameni, Aspronisi, and Christiana. Within the inhabited islands, you can find several major settlements which include Fira, Oia, Emporio, Kamari, Perissa, Imerovigli, Pygros, and Therasia.

Volcanic Eruption

While there are definitely lots of interesting things relating to Santorini, the fact of its creation is perhaps the most important thing to consider. It was built overtime as a volcano is slowly and repeatedly constructed around the sides. When the caldera or the top portion eventually collapsed inwards, the remaining land formed what is now the famous Santorini.

You can probably picture a volcano and easily imagine the topmost portion being shaved off, representing the collapsed part of the mouth. However, you'd think that the main town of Santorini would be located on the bottom-flat surface, which isn't the case at all. The town is situated on the top portion – which is why you'll find that almost all hotels offer a bird's eye view of the Aegean Sea – that's perfectly natural considering the elevation of the town itself.

Now you'd probably want to ask – is there a chance of another volcanic eruption happening on Santorini? While the volcano in Santorini is dormant, it's not exactly inactive. Hence, there's still a chance of the volcano erupting at some point in time. The question is: when? There are a group of scientists today that are tasked with the constant monitoring of Santorini's volcano so that if it eventually happens, it would be easy to warn people about it.

Of course, that's not something you have to worry about during a vacation in the area.

SANTORINI - GREECE

Villages and Towns

There are actually lots of towns in Santorini, each one capable of offering you something unique. While you might not be able to visit all these villages, it helps to find out which ones offer you the activity you want.

Fira – situated on the top of the cliff, Fira offers a spectacular sunset on a daily basis. It's the center of Santorini, especially during the tourist season when all the visitors flock to the village for some much-needed rest and relaxation. You'll find that most hotels are situated in Fira.

Karterados – around 2 kilometers away from Fira, Karterados is most famous for its unique architecture. While Fira itself offers a series of stunning buildings, Karterados is the places you want to visit for Instagram-worthy pictures.

Oia or Ia – a place you should definitely visit for its sunrise or sunset, Oia is perched on top of the caldera. Of course, you can watch the sunrise or sunset anywhere on the island, but Oia is definitely the best place to be in for those events.

Kamari – best known for the black pebble beach, this particular village is situated on the lower portion of the island. The word "black pebble" is not just a fancy term – the sand is literally done in black pebbles resulting from the volcanic eruption.

Imerovigli – just a few minutes away from Fira by bus, this small town is also known for its sunsets and sunrise. If you can't go to Oia, you'll have just as much fun in Imerovigli.

Pyrgos – this is the highest point on the island, containing beautiful monasteries that looks good from any angle. Most people say that Pyrgos can compete with Oia when it comes to sunsets.

Firostefani – a 10-minute walk away from Fira, you can easily visit the village and take advantage of its unique view of the volcano.

Perissa – most famous for its beaches and fish taverns

Akrotiri – make sure to visit this village as it features an archaeological site, giving you a better look at Santorini's roots. The village also contains a Venetian Castle with an amazing view of the sea and sand below.

Monolithos – this is actually a beach with several taverns where you can sit down and relax. The beach itself is shallow so you can easily bring the family over and relax knowing that the kids can play safely.

Megalochori – this traditional village is home of Cycladic churches done in whitewashed colouring.

Vlichada – a small village with its own quiet little beach.

Famous For

It stands to reason that Santorini is a favorite for tourists. Ranked as one of the top islands in the world by Travel+Leisure Magazine, the US News, and even the BBC – it's estimated that the island welcomes a total of 2 million tourists on an annual basis.

But what exactly can you find in Santorini that makes it worth visiting?

The sea, sun, and the picturesque view are the primary reasons why people go there. The towns are built in such a way that you can't help but marvel at how vibrant all the shapes and colors are. People who visit Santorini primarily want to kick back and relax, allowing their body to take in the sun and breathe in the smell of the sea. There are also catamaran trips, so tourists can lounge in the middle of the Aegean Sea for some much-needed unwinding.

Other aspects of Santorini famous with the locals include the thriving Wine Industry and the Architecture.

The Wine Industry is limited but well noted by the wine connoisseurs. There are numerous types of grapes growing in the area, all of which are resistant to diseases – possibly due to the unique soil of the island. Hence, there was no need to replace the vines during the 19th century epidemic – which is probably why these old vines are capable of producing sweet, plump grapes. There are also white wines being produced in the island, known for their citrus and light frankincense aroma. Again, this can be attributed to the unique volcanic soil of the island. While the weather isn't exactly built for wine growing, Santorini wines are respected all over the world and are protected through the Vinsanto and Santorini OPAP designations. Typically, grape yields in the island are only equal to 10 or 20 percent of what is commonly produced in California or France.

The architecture of Santorini is the one thing that will definitely stand out once you visit the island. It's the primary reason why Santorini may be visited all year round. While the sea and wine is seasonal – the architecture looks good no matter what month of the year you decide to visit.

The houses are cubical, made of local stones with their distinctive whitewashed coloring. Set against the hot Greek sun, the resulting imagery is wonderfully striking and unique. In fact, it's easy to recognize Santorini pictures from the architecture alone. The houses built on the precipice of a cliff are small but actually larger inside. Weather-wise, they're perfect because the homes are cool in the summer and warm during the winter.

2

Best Time to Go: Weather and Safety in the City

Santorini is such a beautiful place with an excellent weather that there's really no "bad time" to visit the island. The fact is that any month will be a good time, but if you want a "great" time, then you'll have to take your personal circumstances into consideration. In this Chapter, we'll talk about the different "purposes" for visiting Santorini and the months that will serve your purpose best.

If you Want to Avoid All the Tourists – Visit in January to March

January and February are the off-peak seasons – which means that you'll be able to avoid the crush of people in the airport, the bus, the beach, restaurants, and galleries. There are several tourists, but the place will be yours for the most part. Hence, if you hope to take as many solo pictures as possible – this is the best time for it! This also means you'll be paying less for the accommodation as hotels do their best to get in more people during the off-peak season.

The downside is that many of the shops or hotels won't be open as some of them operate only during the high-tourist season. You might also find it harder to visit famous coffee shops and restaurants because they may not be operating.

Come March, the number of tourists will significantly increase – but not so much that you'll have to worry about the crowd. During this time, there should only be 20% of the average tourist numbers during peak season. Hence, the hotels will still have sufficient slots with prices that are relatively cheaper than the peak months.

If the Crowd Spurs You On – Visit from April to October

These are the peak season months with the crowd density anywhere from 70% to 100% with the ultimate peak happening on the months of July and August. Hence, if you're not really a fan of crowds but still want to enjoy all the tourist attractions, you should choose either May or October where the tourist percentage is around 70% only. The upside is that all the tourist attractions will be open. Restaurants will have their doors wide open and coffee shops will offer all their best delicacies. Shops will be packed with souvenir items and so on.

The downside is of course, the prices will be a little higher compared to the off-peak season. You'll also have a harder time booking a hotel because despite the amount of hotels in Santorini, the number of tourists is even more compelling. If your Santorini vacations fall under any of these months, then make sure you've got advanced booking on a hotel – otherwise you might find yourself spending more for a room for the night.

If You Want Warm Weather and Lounging on the Beach

If you're visiting Santorini for the white sandy beaches, the best months to go would be anywhere from June to September. Incidentally, this also falls within the peak season because a lot of people want the warm weather of this beautiful island. Should that stop you? Of course not! If you plan your holiday right, a peak-season visit shouldn't be a problem. From June to September, the beaches are open, and you can happily swim on the sea and wear summer dresses all day. Before or after these months, the cold season kicks in and the swimming is no longer a good idea. You can still chill out on the beach if you want – but you might want to put on several layers to help with the cold.

If You Want a Packaged Tour

Tours are often offered depending on the best time for their availability. The contents of the packaged tours vary depending on the travel agency that offers them. For the most part though, the tours are any of the following:

- Sunset Sailing Cruise in Caldera
- Luxury Catamaran Day Cruise
- Santorini Sunset Wine Tour
- Santorini Private Tour
- Santorini Photography Tour

These are often offered during the peak season from the late par of May up to the early days of October. The Wine Tour and the Photography Tour can be availed up to November but in truth, the island as so many photo-worthy places that you can walk around and find a subject every few minutes.

If You Want to go Sightseeing

Sightseeing doesn't necessarily require warm weather. You just want a pleasant weather that allows you to walk around and take in all the beauty of this island. If this is your goal in Santorini, then the months of March, April, May, October, and November would be perfect. It's not too cold to walk around in your best comfortable clothes although you might want to pack some items in anticipation of a slight drizzle.

So let's break this down on a monthly basis. Here's what you can expect when visiting Santorin depending on the month.

January
- Tourist: January is an off-peak season month so there will be fewer tourists
- Weather: Still a little cold, you wouldn't want to go sunbathing at this time.

February
- Tourist: Another off-peak season, you can expect to have most of Santorini all to yourself.
- Weather: Still cold, but you can opt for sightseeing and photography tours.

March
- Tourist: During the latter part of March, you should be able to notice a slight increase in the number of tourists.
- Weather: The weather is set to get warm starting from this month, but it's still not a good idea for swimming.

April
- Tourist: By April, there will be a sharp increase in the amount of people in the island.
- Weather: Still cold but definitely better than the previous months of the year.

May
- Tourist: Tourist numbers should reach around 70% of the maximum at this point.
- Weather: The weather starts to become warmer and the beach begins to open up to visitors.

June

- Tourist: With the warm weather a certainty, you'll find that the number of tourists will remain extensive.
- Weather: Warm weather. You can visit the beach at this point.

July

- Tourist: Still packed, the island will start to liven up with all the tourists streaming in from all over the world.
- Weather: Wonderfully warm, you can lounge on the beach and do some sunbathing.

August

- Tourist: This is the ultimate peak month – which means that the

number of people can be anywhere from 100 to 110 percent.
- Weather: The warmest point of this island, August gives you the chance to enjoy everything on the island.

September
- Tourist: Another peak season. Make sure to book your rooms and restaurants as early as possible.
- Weather: Warm weather makes for perfect boat tours.

October to December

- Tourist: Everything winds down at this point. The tourist numbers are starting to go down as the weather turns colder.
- Weather: While boat tours and lounging on the beach aren't good options anymore – you'll find that there are lots more you can do in the island.

3

Safety Tips to Keep in Mind

Santorini is a relatively safe city with few pickpockets or snatchers who might get your valuables as you stroll around the city. Typical safety measures such as having your passport kept in a vault are recommended during your stay here. Weather-wise however, here's what you should keep in mind:

- Always put on sunscreen, especially during the summer months of Santorini. While the hot weather is one of the reasons why people visit the island, very few really appreciate the impact of the hot, Greek sun. A bottle of SPF30 sun screen should always be in your bag. This should cost around 20 Euro.
- Bring a hat and shades for protection all the time. Your sun block will provide for several hours of protection, depending on its SPF.
- The cliffs and low walls can be quite tempting to children but can cause danger, especially with the steps. The same problem may be present for elderly tourists so it's best to skip these areas unless you're absolutely sure of the save.

- Cave exploration is also a wonderful activity in Santorini. Note though that all caves come with a predetermined path that should be followed at ALL times. Deviating from the path can lead you to unstable grounds, thereby causing an accident.
- Stray dogs are quite common in Santorini. Although many of them are friendly, there are those that can be hostile – especially when it comes to food. Don't be alarmed if these dogs decide to follow you around – especially during a hiking trail. They've been known to do that, often trailing people from one village to the next.

4

Transportation To, From and Around Santorini

If you're coming in from other countries, then you should know that Santorini only has one international airport known as the Santorini Thira Airport located north of the Kamari Village. It currently accommodates Olympic Air, Aegean Airlines, and Ryanair as well as chartered and scheduled flights.

It is estimated that the airport handles roughly 2 million passengers every year.

So you have several options for reaching Santorini which includes the following:

- Any Country to Athens to Santorini by Plane or Ferry
- Any Country to Thessaloniki to Santorini by Plane or Ferry
- Direct International Flight to Santorini

Any Country to Any Part of Greece

There are two popular landing spots in Greece that you can use as a main jump off point to Santorini. This is Athens and Thessaloniki. Both have state of the art, international airports the offer connecting flights to the island.

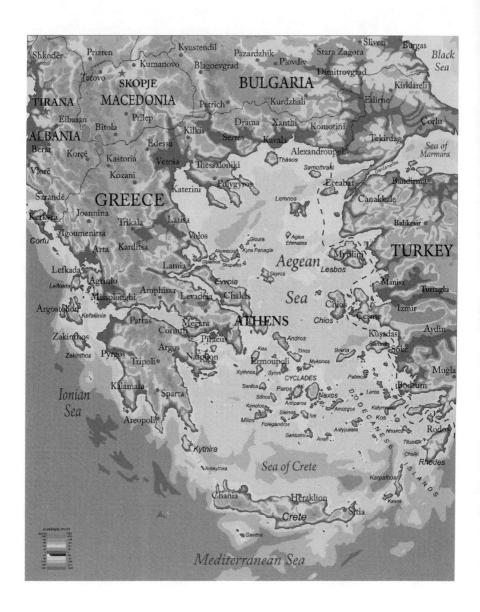

From Any Part of Greece to Santorini by Plane

You'll find that there are several possible jump off points from Greece that could help you get to Santorini. Athens is perhaps the most common jump off point because it has lots of incoming international flights on a daily basis. Here's what you should know about the trip:

- Athens to Santorini by Plane – the trip would take about 50 minutes through multiple airlines. Considering the fact that Santorini is a popular destination, this means you can choose from any of the 29 or more flights to the island on a daily basis. The receiving airport is the JTR Airport as already mentioned above.
- Thessaloniki to Santorini by Plane – the flight from this jump off point is a bit longer – but not by much. The actual flight should take 1 hour and 5 minutes. Unfortunately, flights from Thessaloniki to Santorini is limited, averaging at just 4 each day, typically through Ellinair 18 Airlines.

Reaching Santorini by Ferry

- Athens to Santorini by Ferry–the ferry trip would definitely take longer but on the plus side, you can probably enjoy the sea more in this situation. There are two ports in Athens that you can use: Pireaus or Rafina. You can take a bus or taxi from the Athens airport to the port. From there, you can buy a ticket from any of the three ferry services going to Santorini. The ferry trip could be anywhere from 5 hours to 9 hours, depending on the ferry you're taking.

- Thessaloniki to Santorini by Ferry

Public Transportation in Santorini

- Renting a Car – if you want to explore Santorini at your own pace and you're brave enough to do the driving, then you can hire a car directly from the airport. There are actually three companies that offer hire cars and you can book them online even before landing on the island.
- Private Transfer – of course, there's also the possibility that your hotel booking already includes a private transfer that will wait for

you at the airport. If this is the case, then you should have any problem reaching your hotel.

- Taxi Service – a taxi service would be perfect not just for transfer to the hotel but also for your everyday excursions in the city. Note though that taxi services often have a value of more than €20, depending on where you intend to go.
- Bus Transport – you can also make use of bus transportation if you're part of a large group. You also have the option of using the public transportation – again by bus.
- Public Transportation – this is the only mode of public transport in Santorini and is being operated by the KTEL Company. The cost of the fare from the Santorini airport to the main center should be around €2. Since there's only one terminal, you shouldn't have a hard time finding a bus.

Keep note of the following however:

1. You cannot book or purchase a ticket online. You'll have to be there and ready to take the trip in order to get a ticket.

2. Keep in mind that drivers only take cash. They accept EUR currency.

3. On weekdays, you can catch any of the 4 scheduled journeys, the last one leaving as early as 15:10 from the airport. On the weekends however, there are only 3 journeys on the city center, the last one

leaving at 15:40 from the airport.

4. Note that the bus does not run at night or during the afternoon. Fortunately, you can still take a taxi or hire a private car to get around the city.

5. The bus route is: Santorini Airport – Karterados – Messaria – Fira Bus Station.

ATV and Bike Rental

Renting ATVs and bikes deserve special attention here because while they are definitely many of those in Santorini, not all are worth having. Specifically, some rental agencies will talk you into getting old and broken down ATVs or bikes that will likely make it harder for you to move around the city. This is recognized as a scam among the tourists and is best avoided.

Of course, that doesn't mean there's no worthwhile rental agencies in the island. Make a point of reserving only with a reputable ATV company – ideally those with brand-new looking vehicles. Inspect the vehicle first before signing any contract.

Mark's Bikes
Phone:+30 2286 082833

5

Top 5 Affordable Hotels

Santorini derives much of its income from tourism – which is why the island is full of hotels – each one offering an amazing view of the city and the waters. Here are the best hotels in the island according to visitors.

Best 4 Star Hotels

Amber Lights Villas

This 4-star hotel can be found on the Eastern portion of the island. It's less than a mile away from the village of Imerovigli which makes walking around the town easier. Rooms open up to a view of the Aegean Sea with a terrace that whets the appetite every morning. All rooms are air-conditioned, but you probably won't need them thanks to the refreshing air from the sea.

Amenities of the hotel include wireless internet, a hot tub, a private pool, space center, hammam, access to a garden, restaurants, and an on-site bar. Depending on the room you get, you'll have an in-room mini bar, a flat screen, an iPad, a coffee machine and 1 or 2 separate bedrooms. If you're thinking about hiring a private car, then the hotel has more than enough room for free private parking.

All in all, it's a favorite for couples and trips for groups of friends. It's only 3.7 miles away from the Thira Airport with staff that speak both Greek and English.

Phone: +30 2286 036269

Beldevere Hotel

Located at Fira, this hotel offers a magnificent view of the Aegean Sea as well as the caldera of a volcano. Definitely something worth seeing on a daily basis, Beldevere Hotel amps up the experience by giving you the kind room with handcrafted furnishings and traditional furniture. It really sets off the Santorini experience with the added benefit of being walking distance to museums, shops, and the nightlife. Close by is the Villa of Oia and Akrotiri – both of which are frequented due to the amazing views and the even more amazing sunset. There's also the Minoan Town known for being preserved in volcanic ash. This town is actually 3,500 years old!

Additional amenities include living rooms in junior suites and an amazing rain shower found in all units. There's also an outdoor pool, a gym, a bar, and even a 24-hour reception and concierge service. The staff speaks English so requesting anything should not be a problem.

Phone: +30 2286 025650

Cori Rigas Suites

Located on the Fira Cliffs, the Cori Rigas Suites actually offer a series of condos with a view of the Santorini Volcano and the Aegena Sea. While you can definitely enjoy the sea water – weather permitting – you are always welcome to try out their outdoor pool for a quick dip. There are two types of rooms depending on the view: one gives you a look at the Volcano while the other one opens up to a courtyard or a shared terrace looking into the sea. Either option is good and gives you one amazing view from the moment you open your eyes.

The hotel itself is packed with amenities including wireless internet and made-to-order breakfast. You also have the option of getting a massage and anything else you want that's offered through their full-service spa. Staff speaks several languages including Russian, Greek, German, and English. While the hotel is popular with couples, it actually accepts family bookings and even has babysitting services at an additional charge.

Phone: +30 2286 025251

Kalisti Hotel and Suites

Location: Fira, Fira

If you're looking for a combination of the night life and rest, then look no further than the Kalisti Hotel. It's smack in the middle of Fira Town, literally just yards away from the Caldera. Thanks to its ideal location, the hotel managed to set up a sun-lounger terrace and an outdoor hot tub. You can also check out their pool and

They offer a breakfast buffet so you can fill yourself up before spending the rest of the day exploring Santorini.

Facilities include television, wireless internet, and even babysitting services for family groups. Bathrooms come with luxurious toiletries, slippers, and hairdryer. Each room also comes with a standard mini-bar. There's also a pool bar nearby that serves food and drinks all through the day.

Of course, the proximity of Fira Town means that you have the whole village to explore so there's really no need to hang around the hotel itself. There's a whole world to explore outdoors, especially with the taxis and buses only 50 meters away. Families can take advantage of the babysitting services while they book one of the many tours offered like walking tours, horseback riding, diving, hiking, bike tours, canoeing, fishing, and other as weather permits.

Languages spoken by the staff include Italian, French, Spanish, English, Greek, and German.

+30 2286 022317

Modernity Suites

Location: Fira

A favourite in the town of Fira, this particular hotel rests on top of the Caldera, giving you a view unlike any other. The suites are elegant, some of which come with outdoor hot tubs – perfect for couple vacations. This makes it one of the few hotels that's still perfect even if you're visiting during the cold season. To top it off, you'll enjoy a view of the Aegean Sea and the volcano from your balcony – all while luxuriating in the modern amenities the hotel has to offer.

The suites come with built-in sofas, arched walls, a mini-bar, kettle services, built in shower, and a tablet. There's also daily breakfast served directly to your private terrace. If you feel like nibbling on something, there's a snack menu available the whole day. Suffice it to say, Modernity Suites is built to make sure your every whim is met during your vacation.

Staff speak English and Greek.
Phone: +30 2286 036411

Hotel Matina
Location: Kamari Beach, Santorini

Aside from the stunning view of the beach from this hotel, you're given the added benefit of being literally 3 minutes away from the Kamari Beach. Every time you open your hotel room, you'll be greeted by a breath of fresh salt air, whether you decide to go during the cold or the warm season. On the flipside is a garden that you can enjoy regardless of the weather.

The hotel itself hosts a swimming pool and a pool-side bar. There's also a snack bar and for those who want to fill their days with activities, you can book yourself a snorkelling, cycling, hiking, windsurfing, or cycling activity through the hotel itself. Or you can just start in your room and watch television or scroll through your feed through their wireless internet. A family-run hotel, the Hotel Matina is extensive enough that the staff accommodates four languages: Italian, English, Greek, and French.

An added bonus for this hotel is that it's pet friendly! Guests are allowed to bring their pets upon advance notice with no additional charges.

Phone: +30 2286 031491

Hotel Star Santorini
Location: Megalochori

Just 50 minutes away from the caldera, the Hotel is situated in the traditional settlement of Megalochori. All rooms come with balconies that offer an amazing view of the sea or if you prefer, a look at the lush garden beautifully maintained by the hotel staff. The rooms come with cable TV, radio, hairdryer, and a small fridge.

The beauty of Hotel Star is in its simplicity, giving you just enough facilities for a comfortable stay without overwhelming you with too many options. This gives you the chance to really sink into the experience and focus on what you really want to do during your Santorini trip. After sunning yourself at the Perissa Beach which is around 1.91 miles away – you can come back to the fresh water pool and the poolside snack bar. Couples will also love the hot tub in the hotel and upload their favourite pictures through the hotel-wide wireless internet. For families, there's a playground for the younger guests. Wake up every day to a large spread of a breakfast buffet spread out in the hotel's breakfast room.

If you want to explore the town of Fira, the centre is just 3.7 miles away from the hotel. You can also indulge your inner history buff with a trip to
Acrotiri which is just 1.21 miles away.

Phone: +30 2286 081198

Sea Side Beach Hotel
Location: Kamari

Just one minute away from the Kamari Beach, the Sea Side Beach Hotel is aptly named. Despite being literally a stone's throw away from the beach, the hotel comes with an outdoor pool and a hot tub. Built pursuant to the local architecture, the hotel is a beauty in itself with a decidedly modern interior packed with air conditioned rooms and free wireless internet.

The hotel offers a breakfast buffet to get your day started the right way. From the restaurant or even your own hotel room, you can enjoy the sea view while savouring the sumptuous dishes on offer. There's also an on-site tavern that provides local Greek dishes. If you just prefer to laze around with aromatic coffee, there's a coffee shop on-site too.

Through the hotel, you can book several activities including water sports, diving off-site, hiking off-site, canoeing, and snorkelling. You can also have the hotel arrange a car rental to take you to the centre of Fira for a much-needed nightlife with the locals or some shopping.

The staff is trained to speak English, Greek, and Italian so you can always communicate exactly what you want.

Phone: +30 2286 033403

6

Top 5 Restaurants and Coffee Shops

Top Rated Restaurants in Santorini

Selene Restaurant, Pygros

Originally established in Fira, this Michelin Star Restaurant recently moved to Pygros and managed to maintain its exquisite food all the way. The new location definitely added to the ambience as the restaurant offers a terrific view of the sprawling city, mountains, and the horizon. It's the perfect place for a romantic dinner – or lunch if you're in the mood for it. Ranked as one of the best restaurants in Santorini, Selene is known for their tasteful servings of Greek cuisine. If you really want to make the most out of your Santorini experience, then you should definitely try out signature dishes offered from this restaurant which includes any of the following:

- Suckling Pig – a small portion of pork cooked with potato foam and served with potato peel chips. The pig is thickened with wine, brawn, pita bread, baked onion, tomato jam, and garlic butter.
- Lamb with Trahana – the lamb is cooked with liver, butter of Greek coffee, and powdered porcini. The cream of sour Trahana adds to the overall flavour and gives it the tender lamb meat a distinctive taste.
- Quail – legs of quail is served with pureed carrots, gelee of beer, poached apple, ketchup, and red Florina peppers
- Spanakorizo – Selene managed to add a twist to this classical cuisine. Typically, Spanakorizo is a combination of spinach, onions, dill, lemon, and rice. However, the restaurant adds leeks, kale, yogurt, sheep's milk, and red-raspberry.
- Octopus Yiouvetsi – made with handmade orzo, grilled octopus, olive pate, truffles, and mushroom chips.

Phone:+30 2286 022249

Nikolas Taverna

Located in Fira, the Nikolas Taverna also goes by the name of "The Cave of Nikolas". They opened up in 1967 and continues to operate until today. They're quite a big hit with the tourists with locals only visiting the restaurant only when they know it's not packed with people. Close to the sea, the Nikolas Tavera offers homemade meals with ingredients that come directly from the family farm – how much closer can you get to natural with that?

This is actually the older tavern in the island – which makes it very easy to find. No need to whip out your smartphone – you can ask any local and they'd point you to the right direction. Due to the high demand however, you'd want to make a reservation – especially if you're visiting during the peak months. The good news is that online reservations are welcomed.

Some of the food items on offer include but are not limited to the following:
- Old Time Moussaka – this is the restaurant's most famous dish, providing you with the chance to sample the entire island in a single plate. The product contains fresh ingredients of eggplant, potato, zucchini, chloro cheese, pepper, mzithra, tomato sauce, basil, and minit.
- Lamb Stew in the Pot – tender lamb mixed with organically grown vegetables.
- Fava Risotto with Seafood – combined with seafood and rice

Phone:+30 2286 082303

Kapari Wine Restaurant

A restaurant with the kind of view made for Instagram, the Kapari Wine Restaurant offers not just a gastronomical experience but also access to some of the best wines available in the island. Quick and easy to find thanks to its accessible location, you shouldn't have any problem hiring a private car to take you to the location. Google Maps should also be very helpful at this point and if you're anywhere within the town, you might be able to walk your way to the restaurant.

Kapari Wine is primarily famous for its black risotto, cheese pie, chocolate mousse, and lamb. Note that Kapari Wine Restaurant forms part of the Kapari Natural Resort which also makes for a great hotel to stay in. Just make sure to watch out during the peak season because this restaurant can be quite packed.

Phone:+30 2286 021120

Pitogyros

Located at Oia, the restaurant isn't exactly a restaurant. Don't expect all the bells and whistles in this restaurant because Pitogyros is a grill place packed with genuine Greek street food. It's as authentic as you can get to Santorini's flavours without having a full blooded local cooking for you in a family setting. The restaurant itself is fairly small – which is why you'll need to get there as early as possible to get the few stands available.

The reward though is amazing as Pitogyros is considered to have the best gyros and souvlakia in Santorini. If you feel like there's not enough room for you, then just take out some of the food and bring them to your hotel. There's no reservation here as the grill house is as casual as it gets. It might take some waiting time during the peak season, but if you show up – then you'll surely be fed.

Phone:+30 2286 071119

Koukoumavlos

Another favourite in the area, Koukoumavlos rated well in tripadvisor – and for a very good reason! Their signature dishes include the carpaccio and scampi with spiced apple, white chocolate sauce, and caviar. The restaurant is famous for offering traditional Greek dishes with a twist – while at the same time giving guests the option for something more familiar.

+30 2286 023807

Katharos Lounge

Another cool restaurant to visit with multiple vegetarian options, the Katharos Lounge isn't exactly close to the sea and horizon. In fact, there's very little to see from their current location. Of course, if you visit during an opportune time, you'd find that the location can be quite compelling and stress-relieving. But what makes this a popular one in Santorini? It's one of the few restaurants with a menu for vegetarians. If you're a vegan or just want to make sure you stay in shape during your vacation, then the Katharos Lounge would be a good bet.

+30 697 096 6754

Top Rated Coffee Shops

Coffee Island

Arguably one of the best coffee shops in Santorini, Coffee Island is a favourite not just by the tourists but also by the locals. Located at Agios Athanasios Thiras, the coffee shop is popular enough that you can reach it by asking around the locals. You can also ask your hotel's front desk for directions or really – just use Google Maps because the area is wonderfully indicated through Google.

They serve all kinds of coffee from hot to cold, espresso, Greek coffee, iced tea, and hot tea. They also offer packed coffee beans so if you ever find one that you love, you can easily buy a pack and take a bit of Santorini home with you. While the coffee shop doesn't accept online orders, you can easily check their website and pick a favourite even before you enter their store.

Phone:+30 2286 036330

218 Café

Located in Oia, the 218 Café is popular for its rooftop location that makes coffee drinking a pleasurable experience. This isn't like your local Starbucks where you can grab and run coffee. No, every sip here is an experience in itself as you enjoy the setting sun over the horizon. Perched right on the rim of the caldera, it's one of the best places to end the day after a hectic time at the beach.

Phone:+30 2286 071801

Mylos Café

Located at Firostefani, the café has the unique feature of being built around a windmill. In fact, the word Mylos means windmill and thus, so high up that you can easily see a vast view of the Santorini waters. The café is set up in such a way that you can comfortably rest your back against the pillows and sip coffee – whether hot or cold, strong or creamy. It can be quite crowded during the high season so you'll have to get there pretty early if you want the best seats.

Phone: +30 2286 025640

Skiza Café

Situated in Oia, it's not surprising that Skiza is famous with the locals and tourists. This isn't just a café but also functions as a cafeteria, displaying excellent pastries freshly baked on a daily basis. There are two floors comprising Skiza with the patio being a particular favourite for many. Go here during the late afternoon and you'll be treated to a stunning view of the sun and sea – complete with the cool breeze, compliments of the high altitude of the café building.

Phone: +30 2286 071569

Francos

Located at Pyrgos, the café is also situated near the cliff, thereby giving you a stunning view of the sunset. The café itself is excellent, built primarily for those who want to sit back and enjoy their coffee. A lounge café, Francos serves all kinds of drinks done in the traditional Greek way or if you prefer something a little creamier, they have those too!

Phone:+30 2286 033957

7

Best Museums and Art Galleries

Top Museums

Megaro Gyzi Museum

Founded in 1980, this museum is home to relics and depict the cultural background of Thira. This was originally a family mansion during the 17th century and was able to survive major damage during the 1965 earthquake. Inside you'll find authentic engravings, paintings of Santorini, old photos, and historical manuscripts.

Phone: +30 2286 023077

Wine Museum

If you can't go on a Wine Tour, you might as well visit the Wine Museum featuring the history and life of wine as far back as 1660. The museum is quite unique in that it is situated inside a cave, keeping the temperature cool even during the warm season.

Phone: +30 2286 031322

Lignos Folklore Museum

Built in 1861, the museum was an old winery that's a combination of wine memorabilia, artworks, manuscripts, books, and even a cavern that shows exactly how the volcanic eruption affected the ground.

Phone:+30 2286 022792

Museum of Minerals and Fossils

Offering numerous displays of minerals and fossils, this Museum in Perissa has garnered global attention due to its unique displays. The museum puts emphasis on how the island of Santorini is connected to the world by virtue of old fossils and animals found in its landscape.

Phone:+30 697 640 3771

Naval Maritime Museum

A restored mansion of the 19th century, the museum focuses on the navy and what the Thirans did to contribute to the war time defence of Greece. If you're a fan of various equipment, you'll find here sailing vessels, photographs, models, and Thiran ships.

Phone:+30 2286 071156

Best Galleries

Art Space

A combination of art plus wine making, Art Space is a quick stop but comprehensive – especially with the right guide. In here, you can buy bottles of wine even as you appreciate the age-old method of wine making. This was one of the few first wine producers in the island.

Phone: +30 693 289 9509

Oia Treasures of Art Gallery

Offering a massive array of Greek contemporary art, it's tough not to appreciate the bold colours on display in this gallery. The exhibits are intact but pleasing to the senses – a quiet place to be if you want to bring back the balance during your trip. If you go during the off-peak season, there's also a good chance you'll have the place all to yourself.

Phone:+30 2286 072148

Art of the Loom

Containing oil paintings, ceramics, jewellery, glass, and bronze items – the Art of the Loom Museum is a study of beauty in every corner. In fact, the building itself is a work of art, originally intended as a winery in 1866. The spot managed to retain its structural integrity after that 1956 earthquake and was renovated only in 2010 into its current condition.

Phone: +30 2286 021617

MATI Art Gallery

MATI primarily exhibits the work of a single artist: Yorgos Kypris. He's a sculptor known worldwide for his work on human behaviour and managing to mould them into artistic expressions. Despite the fact that all the items on display only come from one artist, there's no question that the range of creations is mind blowing.

Phone: +30 2286 023814

Mnemossyne Gallery

Imagine the whitewashed exterior of Oia buildings but indoors. This is what the gallery looks like as it opens its doors to visitors all year round. This is the place you want to be in if you want to find a bundle of local artwork by local artists. From jewellery to fine art photographs – the gallery gives you an added appreciation for beauty. It also has an idyllic location because it's only a stone's throw away from the sunset spot of Oia.

Phone: +30 2286 072142

8

Top 5 Bars and Night Clubs

The island may seem like an introvert's dream during the day, but the Santorini social life is actually packed – especially come night time. Following are the top bars and night clubs in the area:

Top Bars

Tranquilo Beach Bar
Location: Perissa Beach

Perfect for chilling out, this beach bar is a favourite among singles and couples alike. They offer cocktails as well as veggies to keep partying all night without worrying about the extra calories. Perhaps their best event is the Latin party where you can dance the salsa from sunset to sunrise.

Phone:+30 2286 085230

Wet Stories Beach Bar
Location: Perivolos Beach

With lounge chairs, sunbeds, and giant bean bags, you'll find this beach bar the ideal location for a group's night out. They serve fancy cocktails as well as beer and offer mainstream music all through the night. This makes the spot perfect for fun conversations with your friends. They offer beach volleyball facilities – so you can burn off the alcohol even as you get drunk.

Phone:+30 2286 082990

Theros Wave Beach Bar
Location: Vlychada Beach

This one's not as packed as the rest – and that's actually the best part. This is because the Theros Wave Beach Bar was built for couples –

hence the ultra-romantic setting. In case you don't know, this beach is also known alternatively as the White Beach. While it's primarily a bar, they also serve exquisite food – perfect for honeymooners.

Phone:+30 2286 112015

Casablanca Lounge Cocktail Bar
Location: Fira

While beach bars are fun, you should also check out the bars offshore. They host excellent parties with the whole shebang of DJs playing funk and soul music. This cocktail bar is perfect for all kinds of visitors, whether single, couples, or groups. Due to the fact that it's located at Fira, the floor is always packed – especially in August.

Phone:+30 2286 027188

Two Brothers
Location: Fira

Dubbed as a party bar, this is the place you want to be if you love to get up and dance. The place has shisha set up all over the place – allowing you to chill, drink, and dance in that order. Ideal for singles who want to meet someone during their summer in Santorini, the dance floor and music is constantly encouraging you to let loose.

Phone: +30 2286 023061

Top Night Clubs

Enigma Club

A pillar of Santorini's nightlife, Enigma has been around for as long as Santorini has been a favourite. Inside, you can dance your heart out or you can choose to sit in the small balcony and just savour the night air. Either way, you're going to get a slice of the unique Santorini taste.

Phone: +30 2286 022466

Koo Club

When it comes to most popular club in Santorini, there are really only two names competing for the top spot: that's Enigma Club and the Koo

Club. If you want to experience night life in the island, you have to hit at least one of these Clubs. Koo Club has an indoor room and an outdoor spot for dancers – three bars dotting the place to keep you filled up with drinks.

Phone:+30 2286 022025

Night Flight

Found at Avis Beach in Kamari, the Night Flight Club opened only in 2015 but is already a popular spot – especially for the locals. Set by the beach, you have the option of socializing indoors or taking a romantic walk by the shore. They serve cocktails and food in a completely casual atmosphere.

Phone: +30 2286 032034

Town Club

Located in Thira, the Town Club is a favourite for the younger visitors of Santorini – as well as the younger locals. The Club hosts events practically on a nightly basis – which means that there's always something new when you drop by.

Phone: +30 2286 023675

Mamounia Club

Hey, if you're looking for traditional Greek music to dance to – then this is the place you want to be. Despite the local music however, the club itself is designed in ultra-modern glasswork with bright coloured palm tree designs that throws an amazing shade all over the place.

Phone: +30 698 297 0799

9

Best Famous Landmarks in the City

In the interest of keeping your options fresh and open, this Chapter will talk about the top landmarks in Santorini without taking in consideration the other places that's already been mentioned. What does this mean? Well, for example – we've already talked about the Selene Restaurant in the later Chapter and while Selene is definitely a Santorini landmark, we're not going to discuss it here to avoid repetition.

So aside from the top bars, clubs, museums, galleries, and restaurants previously discussed – what other landmarks does Santorini have that bears remembering?

Here are the top 5 that every local should know:

Profit Ilias

This is official Santorini's highest peak – which means that you'll be getting the best vantage point of the sunset or sunrise from this area. The Mt. Profit Ilias is measures at 584 meters and at the peak, you'll find that Profitis Ilias Monastery. It's open to the public so you can walk in and marvel at the brilliance of architecture and the difficulty of opening such a building on the top peak. Fun fact: the monastery was a site for one of the many secret schools that ran during the Turkish period.

Ancient Thira

Ancient Thira dates back as early as the ninth century BC and is home to Hellenistic Temples.

They're already in ruins, but that shouldn't stop you from being able to appreciate the landscape that's littered with stone structures. Imagine – hundreds of years ago, these were dwellings where ancient people lived, walked, and breathed.

There's nothing quite like feeling an attachment to the past by touching the same stones children probably drew on during the 9th century.

Caldera

The caldera is in itself a landmark of Santorini – although in reality, the caldera defines the city. It's basically a depression which resulted from the volcanic eruption. The size of the caldera gives you a fairly good idea of how big the volcano was – and how powerfully it erupted at the time.

It ranks as one of the top landmarks in the world and you don't have to pay anything to get there. The spot is open to the public for free at all times – and if you have a hotel in Oia, then you're basically next door neighbours with the caldera!

Lighthouse

Found in Akrotiri, the lighthouse is a coastal tower that's been the subject of one too many photographs. It can be because of the whitewashed walls, the striking tower on top, or the fact that no one's ever been inside – but the tower is a strong highlight of any Santorini visit. Why can't you go inside? The lighthouse is operational and under the control of the Greek Navy, which only adds to its attraction.

Old Port

Every local knows where the Old Port is and can easily lead you to the location. With the cable car, you can reach this landmark quickly which can also be a jump off point to other landmarks of Santorini. While still in use, the Old Port has a very traditional feel to it and with the addition of several shops along the way, you can buy the odd knick knacks for people at home.

10

Things You Can Only Do in Santorini

When visiting a new place, you'd always want to do something that's completely unique in that area. That way, you can always have a unique memory for your vacation. So what exactly is unique in Santorini? Here are the top 5 activities that should tell you exactly what you want to include in your itinerary:

Swim in the Red Beach

Since the Red Beach was already discussed in previous Chapters, it only bears repeating that the Red Beach is an experience you can only have in the island.

Most beaches are done in white sand – but the Red Beach will offer you a wide range of colours in red and rose. It's a unique setup due to the remnants of the volcanic eruption on the island.

Oia Village Visit

When you see pictures of Santorini with the whitewashed buildings and vibrant blue tops – you're seeing an image of the Oia Village.

Know that: (1) there's no other place like it in Greece and (2) the reality of the villages are more amazing than they appear on the photos. Take your time and stroll through the place, all the while taking pictures. Maybe wear something dark or blue to add some startling contrasts to your pictures.

Local Fava Beans

They say half of the reason people travel is for the food – which is why yo should definitely taste dishes that are uniquely served in the area. The local fava beans fit this need to a T.

Akrotiri Archeological Site

Learn a little bit of history while you travel through this archaeological site. Again, this has been discussed in a previous Chapter so the mention of the site is really just a reminder of what you should aim for during your Santorini vacation.

Phone: +30 2286 081939

The Amazing Sunset

It might sound unfair to include sunsets in this list considering how every sunset is unique. However, there's something quite breath-taking about the Santorini sunset.

Maybe it's because when viewing the sunset, you're basically on top of a cliff – giving you a better vantage point as opposed to viewing it from below. Either way, you should definitely leave some time during dusk to just sit back and take in the setting horizon.

Shopping at Epilekton

Found at Oia's Central Square, it's tough to visit Santorini without bringing a little bit of it back with you. This can be done through Epilekton which offers a wide range of art pieces and handicrafts. The Central Square itself is a miasma of shopping finds, giving you the chance to jump from one spot to the next as you inspect possible souvenirs for your trip. Keep your valuables close though – while Santorini is relatively safe – you'd want to make sure you're not losing anything valuable.

Phone: +30 2286 071686

11

Here's Your 3-Day Travel Itinerary for Santorini

With so much things to do and places to see in Santorini, the amount of time you spend may not be enough to fully explore the island. This is why it's a good idea to plan your trip ahead of time so you can hit the highlights of the island and come home with unique memories of this beautiful Greek place. In this Chapter, we'll talk about your ideal 3-day itinerary for Santorini and which places and what activities are best done during your time there.

Day 1

On Day 1, we're going to assume that you arrived in Santorini during the morning and will therefore start exploring in the afternoon. That should give you more than enough time to rest and relax before checking out this wonderful island. So what do you do on your first day? Now, keep in mind that your tour will largely depend on the location of your hotel or which village you're staying in. Fortunately, Santorini is small enough that you can actually go from one village to the next without too much lost time.

Wine Tour

This is perhaps the best thing you can do during your first day. Santorini's wine has won awards and unlike anything else in the world. At the same time, the wine should help you relax after that gruelling trip from Athens to Santorini.

The wine tour usually covers up half the day so you can actually choose this to kick off your Santorini vacation. The wine tour lets you see the wine making process from the ground up. The beauty of this wine tour is that it picks you up from your hotel and then drops you off again – which means that you don't have to worry about transportation on your very first day. You can go exploring on foot if you want to on the next day.

The drop off is equally important because no wine tour is complete without wine tasting. You'll be taken to 3 different wineries in the island and treated to a total of 12 wine styles together with salami, olives, and chees. By the end of the wine tour, you'll be completely relaxed and ready to have your dinner, watch the sunset, and settle in for a full night's sleep.

Tel/fax +30 22860 28358
Mob. + 30 6937 084958

E-mail: info@santoriniwinetour.com

Santorini Sunset

In all honesty, every sunset on Santorini is a sunset worth watching. Thanks to the unique positioning of the island, there's literally no town where the sunset can be termed as bad. Pick your spot and just enjoy the sunset on your first night in Santorini.

Day 2

On your second day, you have the full 24 hours to play with so there are more chances of controlling your schedule.

Here are some of the top places to visit while in Santorini:

Experience Greek Coffee

There's nothing quite the smell of fresh coffee in the morning. While you may choose to taste Greek Coffee in your hotel or opt to visit one of the many coffee shops in the area, Greek Coffee is something you definitely don't want to miss. Make a point of visiting a coffee shop at any point of the day. You're on vacation – coffee shouldn't be limited in the morning!

Red Beach

The Red Beach is the most popular beach destination in Santorini, so it makes sense to check it out. The name is aptly made because the sand is coloured red. The number of people on the Red Beach may vary, depending on whether its peak season or not. Even if you choose not to take a dip however, witnessing the beach itself can already be a big achievement. There's a few beaches in the world with this kind of setup.

Black Beach

Santorini is also known for the Black Beach which – as the name suggests – is covered by a layer of black sand. These come from the volcanic eruption in the past and makes for a striking image in your Instagram. Feel free to take a dip, depending on the weather.

Sunset Boat Tour

Of course, you can also choose to watch the sunset while on a boat. In fact, you shouldn't miss this unique experience. Santorini is famous for its beach and its sunset – the boat tour gives you the best of both worlds in one go. Dinner usually comes with the boat tour, whetting your appetite with the strong smell of salt and sea.

Archaeological Exploration

The problem with a beach exploration is that you can only do it during the warmer weather. If you visit Santorini during the colder climate, you still have other options such as the archaeological tour in Akrotiri. You can go there even without a guide and explore remnants of an ancient civilization at your own leisure. Believe it or not, the remnants here are older than Pompeii but the beauty of the items remain intact. There are guides available as well if you want to appreciate the story behind the relics.

Check out the Local Cuisine

Obviously, you'll visit more than one of the many restaurants discussed above for your meals. Whatever happens, don't forget to visit local eateries or those that serve street food because you don't want to much Santorini in its most authentic flavour.

Souvenir Shopping

Of course, don't forget to do some souvenir shopping around the latter part of the day. Shopping is best done during the first or second day because this gives you the chance to properly pack your stuff.

Day 3

Your itinerary for your third and last day on Santorini would depend largely on when you'd actually leave the island. Ideally, your trip out is early the next morning – which gives you another full day to explore the island. If this isn't the case however, you'd want to pack as much fun in the few hours you have left before you leave for the airport or the ferry.

So what should you do on your third day?

Fira-Oia Hike

There's nothing quite like a relaxing walk from Fira to Oia and then back again, allowing you to explore the caldera along the way. Remember that the caldera is the defining aspect of Santorini so it would be a shame if you couldn't take it all in – especially on your last day. The walk can be quite peaceful .

Photography Tour

If you're not really a fan of a hike however, you can take the Photography Tour on your last day in the island. This is something you definitely don't want to miss because the Photography Tour will give you as much Instagram-upload material as possible. The beauty here is that you'll be with a guide who knows exactly where and how to take your picture so you'll get the best angle in any given image. Memories are great – but fantastic pictures of you will make sure those memories are as amazing as possible.

12

Conclusion

Santorini, Greece is a once in a lifetime vacation experience that deserves a spot in your Bucket List. While there's every chance that you'll visit it again, it makes sense to check out all the prime spots of the islands – just in case you have a hard time scheduling a second visit.

Keep in mind that your itinerary depends largely on your flight schedule, the time of the month of your visit, and your budget. It makes sense to figure out all of these beforehand, so you'll be able to follow a specific strategy while you're on the island. If prepared, you'll find yourself enjoying the experience more as all the worries melt away during this perfect vacation under the hot Greek sun!

SANTORINI - GREECE

13

Thank You

I want to thank you for reading this book! I sincerely hope that you received value from it!

If you received value from this book, I want to ask you for a favour .Would you be kind enough to leave a review for this book on Amazon?

accounting, officially permitted, or otherwise, qualified services. If advice is necessary, legal or professional, a practiced individual in the profession should be ordered.

- From a Declaration of Principles which was accepted and approved equally by a Committee of the American Bar Association and a Committee of Publishers and Associations.

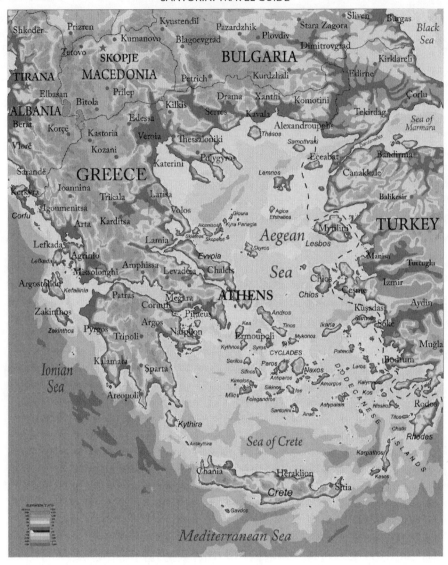

Made in United States
Troutdale, OR
07/31/2024

21678199R10060